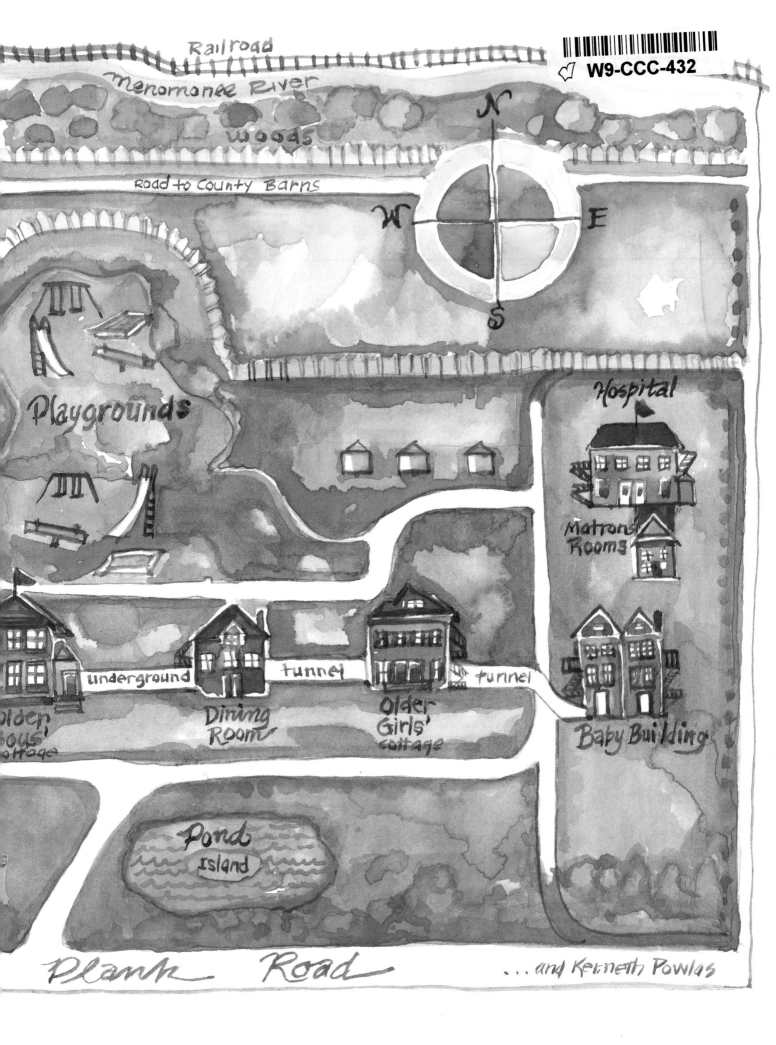

On Her Own

The Life of Betty Brinn

Written by Priscilla Pardini   Illustrated by Joanne Scholler Bowring

Elizabeth A. Brinn Foundation

Acknowledgements

The author gratefully acknowledges the help of: Ray Brinn, Ed Nelson, Becky Nelson, Norman Stefanac, Crystal Stinson Beier, Linda Pohl, Liz Goetsch, Sharon Nienow, Sandra Tunis, Jim Lombardo, Joseph F. Cieminski, Larry Kenny, Paula Kiley, John Stewig, Denise Cassidy, Barbara Tabak, and Sally, Tom and Casey Tolan.

Library of Congress Catalog Control Number: 2001090166
ISBN 0-9711188-0-9

Published by the Elizabeth A. Brinn Foundation, 890 Elm Grove Road, Suite 213, Elm Grove, WI 53122

Dedicated to my parents, Mary and Ben Pardini, who taught me what being a good parent is all about.

– Priscilla Pardini

To: Mari and Tim, Ashley, Tony, Andy, Jerry, Brian – all the artists, musicians, and friends who keep me young and who inspired me throughout the creation of this book. Also, to my husband, Doug, who always has faith in me.

– With thanks and love,
Joanne, "Woman," "Mama"

To all young children who aspire against the odds, and to those generous adults who give them a chance to achieve.

– Elizabeth A. Brinn Foundation

When Betty Brinn was 7 years old, there was one thing she wanted more than anything else in the world. It wasn't a new doll, a puppy or an ice cream cone, things other 7-year-olds wished for. All Betty wanted was for her mother to come to the orphanage where she lived and take her home.

Today, Betty Brinn's name is well known in Milwaukee, Wisconsin. But back in the 1940s, when she was a little girl named Betty Nelson, no one considered her special.

Betty lived at the orphanage with her older sister, Nancy, 9; her brothers, Eddie, 5, and Howard, 3; and her baby sister, 1-year-old Jackie. At night, Betty dreamed that her wish had come true. In the dream, her mother appeared at the orphanage and Betty and her brothers and sisters ran into her arms. Then they all went home and lived happily ever after.

Betty was glad that she had a mother. Some of the children lived at the orphanage because their parents had died and they had nowhere else to go. But even though Betty's mother was alive, she could not take care of her children. Betty's father had left his family, and her mother did not have enough money to pay the rent or buy food, clothes or medicine for five small children.

Sometimes she did not have enough money to take Betty to the doctor. Betty, a smart, pretty little girl, had been born with problems with her back and one foot, and did not walk until she was 3 years old. But Betty was strong, and once she did learn to walk, she walked as well as anyone.

Betty's mother thought the orphanage would be a good home for her children. There, they would be safe, and have plenty of food to eat and clean clothes to wear. And so, in 1945, Betty's mother took her children to the nearest orphanage, the Milwaukee County Children's Home, in Wauwatosa, Wisconsin.

Betty's mother was right. Her children were safe at the orphanage. Women, called matrons, took care of them. They saw a doctor when they got sick. And there were other children to play with. The buildings at the orphanage were old and plain, but the land surrounding the orphanage was beautiful, with rolling hills, woods, big gardens and a pond.

Still, life at the orphanage was not at all like living in a real home. The older children lived in cottages – Nancy and Betty in the girls' cottage, and Eddie and Howard in the boys' cottage. Jackie lived in the baby building.

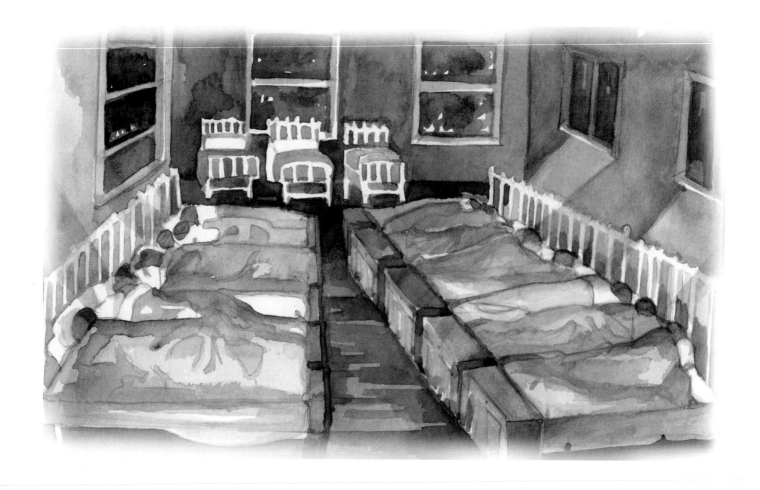

The children slept in huge rooms called dormitories. In the basement, one big room was filled with bathtubs and showers, and another, with toilets. In a third room, sinks stood in long rows. Each child had a comb and a toothbrush, which were kept in cloth pockets that hung on the wall.

Every morning when they woke up, Betty and the other children made their beds. Then everyone got dressed. Each child had two sets of clothes and one pair of shoes. One set of clothes was to wear while the other set was in the wash. When the children wore out their clothes or shoes, or grew too big for them, they got different ones. But the clothes and shoes were never new. They were hand-me-downs already worn by other children and then donated to the orphanage.

The children ate their meals at long tables in the dining room. To get there, they lined up and marched through underground tunnels that connected the cottages to the orphanage's main building. At each table, an older child, called a monitor, was in charge of nine other children. The monitor kept the children quiet and made sure each child got something to eat.

The food at the orphanage was not fancy. The children ate oatmeal for breakfast and a sandwich and piece of fruit for lunch. For dinner, the children usually had mashed potatoes and gravy, and vegetables from the orphanage garden. Sometimes they got a little meat. Once in a while, there was a cookie for dessert.

After breakfast, the older children did chores. Twice a week they stripped the sheets off their beds and got down on their hands and knees to mop the dormitory floor. Each boy also had to scrub another patch of floor somewhere in the orphanage, as well as mow grass, rake leaves and shovel snow. Betty, Nancy, and the other girls worked mostly in the kitchen, washing dishes and peeling potatoes.

After chores, the older children went to the orphanage school. The teachers were serious and strict, and the children worked hard in class. They learned to read, write and do arithmetic. They studied history, geography and spelling. The boys learned woodworking and the girls practiced sewing. Betty was good at math and loved to read.

The children were expected to obey many rules. The most important rule: not to leave the orphanage grounds. Some children would sneak away for a few hours and come back. But other children were so unhappy they tried to run away for good. Almost always, they were caught and brought back. For breaking such an important rule, they got a beating.

The children were also punished for talking in line, spilling their milk, losing their mittens or toothbrush, or disobeying the matrons. Once, when Betty accidentally wet her pants, a matron forced her to sit on the toilet for eight hours.

The children at the orphanage did have some fun. They could play cards or board games or draw pictures in the playroom. On Tuesday nights, if they had been good, they could watch movies. Sliding down the spiral fire escape on the outside of the building was exciting. During the winter, the children played in the snow, although only the boys were allowed to go sledding. The best thing about summer was swimming in the pond.

On occasion, the children got an apple or an ice cream cone. At Christmas each child received a bag of candy. On their birthdays, the children got to pick eight friends to sit with them at the Birthday Table, where they had a special meal: a slice of ham, an egg, bread and butter, a piece of cake, milk and candy. They felt lucky because they did not have to eat vegetables.

Some children were happy at the orphanage. Living there was better than having no home at all. And being taken care of by matrons was better than being on their own. But Betty was not happy. She was sad and lonely. She missed her mother, and did not understand why she could not live in a real home with people who loved her.

Betty also missed her younger brothers and sisters. She saw Nancy every day, but she almost never saw Eddie and Howard. Even at meals or during playtime, the boys and girls were kept apart. Only once in a while did Betty catch a glimpse of her brothers through wooden railings that separated the boys' and girls' playgrounds. The only time she saw Jackie was when the little girl played on the balcony of the baby building.

Betty's dream that her mother would rescue her and her brothers and sisters from the orphanage never came true. The children did leave the orphanage after several years, but not with their mother.

Instead, they went to live with foster families, strangers who took in children who had no homes of their own. The foster parents gave the children food and clothing and sent them to school. In return, the children had to help with the chores.

Many of the foster families that took care of Betty and her brothers and sisters lived on poor farms in northern Wisconsin. But just as at the orphanage, the Nelson children were separated. Betty and Nancy were sent to one foster home, and the three youngest children to another.

Over the next few years, Betty lived in 17 foster homes. Some of Betty's foster parents were kind, and tried to take good care of her. But in many of the homes, Betty was miserable. Sometimes she did not get enough to eat and was forced to work hard, hoeing crops and cleaning barns. Often, her foster parents yelled at her or beat her when she did something wrong. They treated their own children better than they treated Betty.

When Betty was 13, she and Nancy were sent to live with Nellie and Henry Stinson, an older couple who owned an 80-acre farm near the small town of Almond in central Wisconsin. Nellie Stinson was a strict, religious, good-hearted woman. Henry Stinson was a jolly man with white hair. The Stinsons had one grown daughter and two granddaughters living nearby. But they loved children so much that when they heard about Betty and Nancy, they took the girls into their home.

The next three years were happy ones for Betty. The Stinson farm, with its fields, woods, and grove of willow trees, turned out to be a wonderful place. The Stinsons lived in a big, white farmhouse. They also owned a barn, a chicken coop, a pigsty, and a granary where feed for the animals was stored. The family grew hay and planted huge flower and vegetable gardens. Unlike some of Betty's other foster homes, where water had to be pumped by hand and the toilet was located outdoors in an outhouse, the Stinson farm had running water and a modern bathroom.

Betty and Nancy went to school in Almond. After school and on Saturdays, the girls were expected to help with chores, such as weeding the garden and washing dishes. But there was still time to play with the Stinsons' granddaughters, Linda and Betty Ann, and to go shopping at Blaine Store down the road. Every Sunday the Stinsons took the girls to church. Nellie Stinson wanted them to grow up knowing right from wrong.

For Betty, the best thing about living with the Stinsons was being part of a family. She still missed her mother and younger brothers and sister, but she loved Nellie and Henry Stinson. When she grew up she told people they were like parents to her, and that their farm was the only real home she had ever known.

Nellie Stinson taught Betty to cook and bake. Together, they made special meals at Thanksgiving and Christmas, and in the fall when men called threshers came with their huge machines to harvest the Stinsons' oats. At times like these, the long dining room table was covered with platters of fried chicken, mashed potatoes and cucumbers in sour cream dressing.

Henry Stinson became Betty's special friend. He adored the spunky, energetic girl who made him laugh. From Henry, Betty learned how to be a friend to other people. He also taught Betty a little bit about business, helping her set up a roadside stand where she sold vegetables from the garden. To her delight, he let Betty keep the money she made.

Betty was happy at the Stinson farm, but when she was 16 she set out alone for Milwaukee, where her mother lived. By then, Betty was a strong and determined young woman who had learned how to take care of herself. She decided it was time to make her dream come true. Betty moved in with her mother, but their life together was not the way she had imagined it. After years apart, Betty and her mother were strangers.

Still, Betty liked living in Milwaukee. It was exciting to be in a big city. She had fun going to movies and dances, and she loved shopping. As a student at Washington High School, Betty again took charge of her own life. When she did not have a date for the prom, she bought herself a fancy dress and went alone, on the bus.

While still a teenager, Betty got married and before long had a baby boy she named Norman. But soon after Norman was born, Betty's marriage ended, and she got a job at a furniture store to support herself and her son. Betty was young and very poor, and did not have a good education or a family to help her. But she was smart and willing to work hard. And she was determined to make a good life for herself and Norman.

Over the next few years, Betty had lots of jobs. She was an office worker and a switchboard operator. She sewed draperies and sold women's dresses. She liked jobs that taught her new skills. And whatever the job, Betty always did her best.

When she took a job as one of the first women to deliver mail for the U.S. Post Office, she was teased by some of the men she worked with. They said a woman could not deliver mail as fast as a man. That made Betty angry. It also made her determined to prove the men wrong. Her first day, she finished her mail route before any of the men.

The year 1961 was a happy one for Betty. She got married again, to a wonderful man named Raymond Brinn who would be her husband for 31 years. Betty and Ray, who ran a local insurance agency, had three children: Daniel, David and Becky. Betty loved her children and tried to help them the way she wished her mother had helped her. Although she had to work long hours, she never missed her children's ball games or school programs. She taught them to be generous and fair, and told them again and again that if they worked hard and never gave up, they could be anything they wanted to be.

Having four children made Betty think about her own childhood. She remembered the unhappy years she had spent at the orphanage and in foster care. But Betty did not feel sorry for herself or talk much about those times. She just kept trying to make life better for herself and her family.

Because she was good at math, Betty got a job as a bookkeeper at a Milwaukee hospital, keeping track of the hospital's money. She liked that job, and later worked in several doctors' offices. Always curious, Betty asked lots of questions and read many books about health and health care.

Before long, Betty had taught herself so much she was hired to run a new business, Managed Health Services, which helped poor people get good health care. Betty remembered that when she was a young child her mother had not always had enough money to take her and her brothers and sisters to the doctor. She was glad the business helped other mothers and their children stay healthy.

Some of the people Betty hired to work for her were poor women with children. The women had never had jobs before, but Betty did not care, as long as the women worked hard. She knew that if the women had good jobs they would not have to send their children to orphanages or foster homes.

People were amazed when the business began to grow and make money. They knew Betty had never been to college and had four children to take care of at home. But Betty proved that she could do anything. She learned to make decisions and solve problems. She was not afraid to speak up, and if she thought she was right about something, no one could change her mind. If she made a mistake, she learned from it, and never made the same mistake again. People called Betty a tough businesswoman.

Betty made enough money to buy pretty clothes, live in a nice house, send her children to good schools and travel to interesting places. She had lots of friends, and loved to laugh and have fun. One day, she even dyed her hair bright red. Her life now was very different from when she was a child. She felt safe and secure and knew that people loved and respected her.

Betty shared her good fortune. She gave big parties for her family and friends, cooking and baking the way Nellie Stinson had taught her. At Christmas, she held parties for her workers and gave them extra money.

As the business grew more successful, Betty found ways to help poor and neglected children, too. The company gave money to the Boys & Girls Clubs to pay for nurses to help keep children healthy. It also gave money to La Causa Day Care Center to take care of babies whose parents were poor. Betty did not want other children to suffer the way she and her brothers and sisters had suffered when they were young.

In 1992, when she was only 53 years old, Betty died of cancer. Hundreds of people came to her funeral. They talked about Betty's remarkable life. Some of them could not believe that a little girl who had grown up in an orphanage and in foster homes had become such a successful wife, mother and businesswoman.

Betty is gone, but she will never be forgotten. Money from the business she ran helped to pay for Milwaukee's children's museum and the children's room at the Milwaukee Public Library. Today, both of these wonderful places are named for Betty Brinn, a poor, abandoned little girl who proved that anything is possible, no matter how hard one's childhood may be. On her own, with strength, determination and hard work, Betty made a wonderful life for herself and became a true friend to all of Milwaukee's children.

The Stinson
Farm
Almond, Wisc.

Chicken Coop

Anima[l]
Pen

Pigst[y]

Be[]
Go[]